Mary DeTurris Poust

LITURGICAL PRESS

Collegeville, Minnesota

www.litpress.org

Nihil Obstat: Reverend Robert Harren, *Censor deputatus*

Imprimatur: ✥ Most Reverend Donald J. Kettler, J.C.L.,
Bishop of Saint Cloud, Minnesota, May 12, 2015.

Cover design by Monica Bokinskie. Photo courtesy of Thinkstock.

ISSN: 1552-8782

ISBN: 978-0-8146-4954-1   978-0-8146-4980-0 (ebook)

Introduction

The stark and somber season of Lent is upon us, inviting us to enter into the desert with Christ. If we're lucky, we will cross the parched earth of our sin-strewn spiritual lives to find the oasis of God's mercy and love waiting for us on Easter morning, turning our barren interior landscape into a lush paradise. But anyone who's been on the doorstep of Lent before knows that these forty days are fraught with temptations and shimmering mirages that lure us off our path with the promise of pleasure, comfort, ease.

It's good to remember as we begin this journey that it's okay if it is not always a direct route. We are human, after all, and although we sometimes don't seem to grasp that, God does. There will be days when we feel as though we're not making any spiritual "progress" at all, and other times when we seem to be slipping farther and farther from our goal. Fortunately for us, God is kind and merciful. And patient beyond measure.

So breathe deep and just begin. Stake out a daily dwelling place in the heart of Scripture, where you will find guideposts and markers, examples and inspiration to help move you through this season. When you miss a step or lose sight of your plans for fasting, almsgiving, and service, find a quiet spot to refocus your mind and reconnect with the whisper of the Spirit. Away from the chaos and noise of the outside world, you'll be better able to soak up the spiritual nourishment you need to sustain you.

Transformation doesn't come in an instant or all at once. It comes bit by bit and with daily effort. We are blessed to have this season set apart, a time to break from our routine and immerse ourselves in the story of our salvation. Although at Lent we tend to focus on what we are doing for God and for others, the greatest blessing of this season is what God is doing for us.

"Lent is a favorable time for letting Christ serve us so that we in turn may become more like him," says Pope Francis. "This happens whenever we hear the word of God and receive the sacraments, especially the Eucharist. There we become what we receive: the Body of Christ. In this body there is no room for the indifference which so often seems to possess our hearts."

Let us begin the journey together . . .

Reflections

A Beautiful Paradox

Readings: Joel 2:12-18; 2 Cor 5:20–6:2; Matt 6:1-6, 16-18

Scripture:
[R]eturn to me with your whole heart." (Joel 2:12)

Reflection: Every Ash Wednesday, I head to church with a heart and head full of spiritual dreams and goals. *This* will be the year I do Lent right. *This* will be the season I finally get my spiritual act together once and for all. Even as I revel in that hopefulness, I know there's a very good chance I will not live up to my grand plans, that I will fail, maybe even before the first week of Lent is out. How many times have I pulled that same old spiritual bait and switch with God? Sometimes I wonder how I can be so hopeful every Ash Wednesday when I know my own Lenten track record, when I know myself too well.

And yet that is the beautiful paradox of Ash Wednesday: Hope in the most unlikely places. Today's focus on our mortality, that we are dust and to dust we shall return, is beautifully balanced by the promise of resurrection that we know awaits us in the aftermath of Calvary. We will not be forgotten or abandoned.

Our God is "gracious and merciful," we hear in today's first reading, "slow to anger, rich in kindness, / and relenting in punishment." Later, in the Gospel of Matthew, we are told,

"Your Father knows what you need before you ask him" (Matt 6:8). And so we begin our Lenten season, wary of our own weaknesses but buoyed by the strength of God's love. Nothing we do can cut us off from that love. No wonder it's so easy to hope.

Meditation: Do you see Ash Wednesday as a day focused on your shortcomings or as a day that offers you the promise of second chances? Are you willing to return to God with your whole heart this Lenten season, or do you secretly try to hold onto a piece, afraid of surrendering completely? What does surrender look like amid the busyness of daily life? What one thing might make it more complete?

Prayer: Merciful God, we stand before you today, fully aware of our human frailty, but hopeful in your love. We offer you our hearts and all our plans for this Lenten season. You know what we need most to grow closer to you in the days and weeks ahead. Give us eyes to see your path and ears to hear your voice amid the chaos of the world around us.

What Do You Choose?

Readings: Deut 30:15-20; Luke 9:22-25

Scripture:
Blessed the man who follows not
   the counsel of the wicked
Nor walks in the way of sinners,
   nor sits in the company of the insolent,
But delights in the law of the LORD
   and meditates on his law day and night. (Ps 1:1-2)

Reflection: Two out of three children in our family are teen-agers, which means my husband and I spend a lot of time talking about making good choices—the groups they join, the friends they make, the TV shows they watch. It seems obvious to us as parents that the difference between good and bad choices is often quite clear. And yet we can't always see those same distinctions in our own lives.

Today's readings remind us that we have a choice in our destiny. Moses tells us, "I have set before you life and death, the blessing and the curse. Choose life, then, that you and your descendants may live, by loving the LORD, your God, heeding his voice, and holding fast to him."

The choice is usually pretty clear. We know in our hearts the right thing to do, but because of human weakness or peer pressure or simply the consensus of our culture, we often choose the lesser thing.

In the gospel, Jesus puts it another way: "What profit is there for one to gain the whole world yet lose or forfeit himself?" Again, it comes down to choices. Are we trying too hard to "save" our life—through material gains, power plays, the illusion of control—at the risk of losing our soul? Like petulant teens we want immediate gratification, the shiny bauble over the polished stone.

When it comes to choices, the cross is always going to lose out to the crown if we look at things with earthly eyes. God asks us to look through the prism of his love and mercy instead, to choose eternal life over fleeting happiness. The choice isn't always easy, but the choice is always ours.

Meditation: Have you ever willfully risked a break in your relationship with God over something meaningless, or even dangerous? Why is it so easy to see where other people make wrong choices and so hard to see it in ourselves? Do you "hold fast" to God, or are you willing to go your own way even if it means getting lost in a sea of superficial "promises"?

Prayer: Dear Jesus, we know you are the only way to lasting happiness. Give us the courage to do the right thing, to follow where you lead and not where the world would have us go, to choose life over death, blessing over curse, today and always.

The Power of Simple Sacrifice

Readings: Isa 58:1-9a; Matt 9:14-15

Scripture:
They seek me day after day,
    and desire to know my ways. (Isa 58:2)

Reflection: Years ago, I was having lunch with some friends
to celebrate a birthday. It happened to fall during Lent, and
although I quietly passed on the chocolate cake, one of the
women there called attention to it and asked if I was skipping
dessert because it was Lent. I sheepishly admitted Lent was
the reason, at which point she announced to the group that
giving up cake or sweets or chocolate wasn't going to help
anyone, and maybe I should be doing something positive
for someone in need instead. Point taken, but we miss big
opportunities for spiritual and personal growth if we think
giving up simple things has no power to transform us.

In today's readings we hear a lot about fasting, which can
take so many different forms. We can fast from favorite
foods, from social media, from shopping, from morning cof-
fee or nightly wine. While those sacrifices may seem fairly
insignificant on the surface, every single one of those things
can make us more aware of the journey we are on, of people
who have less than us, of the ways we try to fill ourselves
up with things that can never satisfy. Every time we catch

ourselves reaching for that bag of chips or container of ice cream, we are forced to confront our own human weakness and our Lenten promises. And all of that brings us back to the heart of the matter: Jesus.

St. Augustine said that prayer and fasting are the two wings of charity. In other words, we may never find the strength or courage or motivation to serve those in need without the seemingly easier practices of fasting and prayer. So, as it turns out, sometimes a piece of cake is much more than a piece of cake.

Meditation: Without a spiritual focus, fasting is just another version of crash dieting. How are you making your Lenten sacrifices count in a spiritual way? Can you more effectively use the seemingly smaller moments of the season to bring about a larger transformation in your own life and in the lives of those around you?

Prayer: May our sacrifices this Lent help clear out the clutter in our hearts and souls so that you may enter more fully into our lives, dear Lord. Give us the wisdom to recognize sparks of transformation in the prayer, fasting, and charity we practice this season.

A Seat at the Table

Readings: Isa 58:9b-14; Luke 5:27-32

Scripture: "I have not come to call the righteous to repentance but sinners." (Luke 5:32)

Reflection: I vividly remember the year my husband and I served a Thanksgiving breakfast of hard-boiled eggs and tortillas to the day laborers on a corner in Austin, Texas. We were pretty pleased with ourselves for giving up a few hours of our holiday morning, but for the folks from the local Catholic Worker house who carted food to that site day in and day out, this was business as usual. These folks didn't just serve breakfast on that corner every single morning, even in pouring rain and blazing heat; they lived alongside the poor, invited them to their table, welcomed them into their hearts. The homeless, the addicted, the abandoned—no one was turned away because all were recognized as children of God. Even when one among them stole a car from the Catholic Worker house, they lovingly went back to serving breakfast, unfazed by an infraction that might stop the rest of us in our tracks.

In today's gospel, Jesus teaches us that same reality in pretty dramatic fashion when he invites himself to Matthew's house for dinner. Tax collectors weren't just unpopular; they were despised, not only for cooperating with the Roman occupiers, but because they were often corrupt. "I have not come to call the righteous to repentance but sinners," Jesus tells the Pharisees when they question his choice of dinner companions. I'm guessing that many of us put ourselves in the Pharisees' camp—satisfied with ourselves for what we perceive as our righteous and faith-filled lives. But none of us, not even the greatest saints, fall outside the sinner category. We are firmly entrenched there, no matter how much we'd like to believe otherwise. Jesus came to save us all. How blessed we are to be invited to the table!

Meditation: Do you often see yourself on the side of the Pharisees, thinking of yourself as righteous and deserving rather than sinner and saved? Is there someone in your life that you consider unworthy of your time, attention, love? Can you follow Jesus' example and extend an invitation, even if only in attitude and kindness, to that person?

Prayer: Open our eyes, Lord, so that we may recognize you in every person we meet. Open our hearts so that we may love as you love, without conditions, without limit, without expectation of anything in return.

Taunted by Temptation

Readings: Deut 26:4-10; Rom 10:8-13; Luke 4:1-13

Scripture:
When the devil had finished every temptation,
   he departed from him for a time. (Luke 4:13)

Reflection: When my son, Noah, was seven years old, another boy told him he had to perform certain feats—like jumping off the monkey bars from a height—in order to maintain their friendship. My husband and I had to explain that real friends don't ask us to do things that might endanger or embarrass us. It was a hard lesson for a little boy, because jumping off the monkey bars didn't seem like such a big deal. But, if he gave in this time, what demand might come next? Stealing? Cheating? The temptations were only likely to escalate. As adults, we know the power of temptation, in matters both great and small. It's not in our nature to say no when saying yes might make our lives seem easier or more fun or less lonely.

In today's gospel, we see Jesus facing temptations beyond anything we might face. Imagine how tempting it must have been to turn the stones into bread and shut Satan up once and for all. But it wouldn't have shut him up; it would have given him more power. I've always been struck by the last line of this verse: "When the devil had finished every temptation, he departed from him for a time." For a time. He would be back, probably when Jesus was at his weakest. Temptation is like that, always taunting us when we are most desperate or vulnerable. Jesus had been praying and fasting in the desert for forty days when he was tempted. He was "filled with the Holy Spirit." If we ground our lives in regular prayer, we, too, will receive what we need to do battle with the demons that threaten us daily.

Meditation: What are your weaknesses, the things that most often tempt you to stray from what you know is best? Do you attempt to face your temptations on your own, or do you rely on the power of prayer to see you through? When a temptation is getting the best of you, can you reflect on Jesus in the desert, remembering that you are not alone?

Prayer: Gracious God, when we feel ourselves bowing to the lure of temptation, give us the strength and courage we need to turn away from sin and toward you. With you we can be strong.

Lead with Your Heart

Readings: Lev 19:1-2, 11-18; Matt 25:31-46

Scripture:
"You shall love your neighbor as yourself.
I am the LORD." (Lev 19:18)

Reflection: We were sitting around our kitchen table one morning talking about the Ten Commandments. Although that's not typical mealtime conversation for us, on this day something sparked a discussion. One of my children, with the pressure of parental eyes gazing on her, was having trouble getting the exact commandments down.

Once out of the spotlight, however, she rattled off close approximations of nine out of ten, and then said, "Love God, and love your neighbor as yourself." With those words, I was satisfied because she understood the heart of the law even if she was a little shaky on the letter of the law.

Today's readings give us a dose of both. Moses tells us not to take what isn't ours; Jesus tells us to give away what is. And that's what makes the Gospel such a radical challenge.

"Whatever you did for one of these least brothers of mine, you did for me," Jesus says. We take some comfort in that. We think back to the time we gave food to the local pantry, the time we threw extra money in the collection, the time we visited an elderly relative, and we figuratively pat ourselves on the back and think, "We're in."

But then Jesus says, in a sense, "Not so fast." Were there times we could have given but didn't? If so, we were ignoring Jesus himself, who, as Blessed Mother Teresa once said, often comes to us in the "distressing disguise of the poor." Jesus' admonition can be a little disheartening. How can we give to everyone in need?

So much of what Jesus asks of us has to do with interior attitude as well as exterior action. Do we hear of a need and turn a blind eye? Probably not. Do we wish we could do more? All the time. It comes down to a life guided by what is written on our hearts and not just what is written in stone. As Mother Teresa said, "If you can't feed a hundred people, feed just one."

Meditation: Have you hardened your heart toward those in need? Can you find one person, one group, one cause that needs your help and get involved?

Prayer: Dear God, you sent your Son to us cloaked in poverty and humility. Help us to embrace opportunities to live in solidarity with the poor and to learn to live with less so that others may have enough.

February 16: Tuesday of the First Week of Lent

What Prayer Requires

Readings: Isa 55:10-11; Matt 6:7-15

Scripture:
"This is how you are to pray." (Matt 6:9)

Reflection: When I taught fourth- and fifth-grade faith formation, I would try to impress upon the kids that even if they forgot the words to the prayers they learned at home or in class, they could always talk to God. I wanted them to understand that as soon as they felt that urge to move closer to God, they were already praying, whether they said all the words or no words at all.

Sometimes they'd look at me like I was crazy. How could they pray if they didn't know the words? Today, in the gospel, Jesus says, "This is how you are to pray." And then he goes on to give his disciples the words to the Lord's Prayer, the same words that tumble from our lips so naturally. Prayer feels like it should require words, and yet prayer really requires only one thing: a willing heart.

I did an experiment with those same fourth-grade students. One week during Lent I had them sit in silence while I read a guided meditation on the passion. Another week we sat in total silence while we attempted centering prayer. The next year, when those students returned as fifth-graders, I asked them what they remembered most from the year before, and of all the things I had taught them—the commandments and the Mass and "famous" Scripture stories—multiple children raised their hands and said, "The times you had us pray in silence."

Yes, it's important to be able to go to God in prayer with the words that Jesus gave us, but it is also important to go to prayer with no words at all, to go only with the hope of hearing something, to listen not with our ears but with our hearts.

Meditation: Do you put too many parameters on your prayer life, creating too many requirements that must be met before you can pray? How often do you sit before God in silence and let the Spirit do the talking? Can you learn one new prayer or prayer method this Lent?

Prayer: Holy Spirit, guide us in prayer and speak to us in silence. Help us to shut out the noise of the world so that we can hear the still, small voice of God above the din. Give us a heart that listens and a spirit that seeks you through words, songs, and silence.

Following the Signs

Readings: Jonah 3:1-10; Luke 11:29-32

Scripture:
A clean heart create for me, O God,
    and a steadfast spirit renew within me. (Ps 51:12)

Reflection: We like signs, something concrete to let us know we're on the right path. Often in prayer, when we're feeling overwhelmed or desperate, we say, "Lord, send me a sign." Wouldn't it be great to have the spiritual version of a GPS, a "home" button we could push that would find us the shortest route to God?

Sometimes the sign—the best route—is right in front of us, like the flashing purple road map of the GPS showing us exactly where we need to go, but we manage to look away or around it. Not *that* sign. I'll wait for another sign, a better sign. We recalculate our own path, and often end up lost.

In today's readings, God is clear about paying attention to the signs meant to guide us home. The story of Jonah is pretty dramatic. I try to imagine how I'd react if someone came to town preaching what Jonah preached and telling me to repent and reform my life. Would I put on the modern equivalent of sackcloth and ashes, or would I look for a different Jonah, a more palatable sign?

When I imagine the crowds sitting at Jesus' feet, listening to him say that there is "something greater than Jonah here," I try to see myself there, but what I really should be doing is trying to see Jesus here. Now. His words, the sign of his life, are not something meant only for people two thousand years ago but for us today. We seek a sign to lead the way, but Jesus is the Way, no signs or recalculations required.

Meditation: They say hindsight is 20/20. Is that true in your spiritual life as well as your "regular" life? Can you look back and see the times God was gently leading you where you needed to go? How often did you choose to forge your own path rather than follow the nudging of the Spirit? This Lent can you try to become more aware of God's presence in the details of your life?

Prayer: Abba, Father, we know you are there, like a loving parent, trying your best to lead us where we need to go. Give us the grace to recognize the signs you place on our path and to heed your directions, even when they take us to the road less traveled.

Seeking Answers

Readings: Esth C:12, 14-16, 23-25; Matt 7:7-12

Scripture:
"Which one of you would hand his son a stone
    when he asked for a loaf of bread,
    or a snake when he asked for a fish?" (Matt 7:9)

Reflection: "Ask and it will be given to you . . . " That's quite an offer, isn't it? And so often I think we take it at face value. We ask and then hold out our hands, waiting for the answer to slip to earth like candy from a heavenly vending machine. Unfortunately, that's not how it works, and most of us know that from experience. We can ask for things, and the answer we get usually turns out to be very different from the one we wanted. Is God going back on his promise? We're asking; we're knocking; we're seeking. Why won't God follow through?

I think about the time my son asked for an inappropriate video game or my daughter begged to wear makeup when she was far too young. They asked, they begged, they figuratively knocked until I was about ready to open the door against my better judgment, but then I remembered my role as a parent. I know what's best for my children, even when they are convinced they know otherwise. And so it is with God. We may know what we want, but God knows what we need, and it is often only in hindsight that we see the wisdom of not getting our way. That doesn't mean we learn to love every answer, but, little by little, we can learn to see the beauty of the gifts we didn't ask for or even consider. God has a plan. So go ahead, knock, but we should do so trusting that our life is unfolding as it should even if we don't like whatever is waiting on the other side of that door.

Meditation: When you are handed an answer in prayer that goes against everything you had hoped for—an illness not cured, a life not saved, a job not found—can you find a way to trust in God's plan over your own? Can you go to God in prayer and truly open yourself up to his will rather than try to bend God's will to your own?

Prayer: Heavenly Father, help us to let go of our need to be in control, to make life move according to our plans not yours. Give us eyes to see and ears to hear your message so that we might open ourselves up to your possibilities rather than close ourselves off in anger or despair.

What Are You Carrying?

Readings: Ezek 18:21-28; Matt 5:20-26

Scripture:
"Therefore, if you bring your gift to the altar,
   and there recall that your brother
   has anything against you,
   leave your gift there at the altar,
   go first and be reconciled with your brother,
   and then come and offer your gift." (Matt 5:23-24)

Reflection: Anger seems to be a natural by-product of our overscheduled, overstressed society. Whether it bubbles just below the surface in seemingly civilized fashion or explodes without warning for all to see, it is a dangerous thing because it damages the angry person as much as the person on the receiving end. No one walks away unscathed.

In a once-upon-a-time hit pop song, there's a line that says, "You keep carrying that anger, it'll eat you up inside." Isn't it the truth? Scripture gives us a similar message but with spiritual kick and a lot more at stake.

Both the first reading from Ezekiel and the gospel reading from Matthew remind us today that we cannot truly love God if we are carrying around anger toward someone else. In order to be reconciled with God, we must be reconciled with each other. If we have the courage to make amends, what will we find on the other side? Eternal life with God. Even the best pop song can't offer a promise like that.

"But I say to you, whoever is angry with his brother will be liable to judgment," Jesus says. No hidden message there. It's all abundantly clear, and lest we think that's a quaint maxim for a time long ago, Pope Francis has given a similar warning in recent years: "To speak badly of someone else is to kill because it's rooted in the same hatred."

It's easy to recognize hatred as the root of war and murder, but it cuts a little close to the bone when we think of the same kind of hatred fueling our own petty gossip or anger. What disguise does our hatred wear?

Meditation: Are you carrying around any anger or resentment toward a family member, a friend, a coworker or neighbor? What can you do to bring about reconciliation? Has your anger ever made you feel truly better or just avenged or justified? Even if you can't see hatred at the heart of your anger, is it possible that it is present just the same, even if only toward a situation or your own weaknesses?

Prayer: Jesus, Prince of Peace, teach us to build bridges rather than walls, to offer outstretched hands rather than crossed arms, to choose reconciliation rather than retribution, even when we feel justified. Help us see the wisdom in being the first to say, "I'm sorry."

Love Begets Love

Readings: Deut 26:16-19; Matt 5:43-48

Scripture:
"He makes his sun rise on the bad and the good,
and causes rain to fall on the just and the unjust."
(Matt 5:45)

Reflection: A friend of mine posted a Facebook status update recently that suggested that if we had created God instead of it being the other way around, we certainly wouldn't have included the gospel mandate we hear today: "Love your enemies and pray for those who persecute you." True, very true. Of the many difficult gospel mandates we are challenged to live if we want to call ourselves Christian, this is one of the most difficult. We hear it, we know what we're supposed to do, but, when it comes time to actually turning toward someone we consider an enemy and loving him, it can be beyond difficult or flat-out impossible.

Surely, Jesus didn't mean that mandate literally, right? We're only human, after all. There must be a hidden meaning, an easier translation. But this is our truth. Jesus loved *all*, not just some, and not just those who were nice to him, and we are called to do the same, like it or not.

"When you love people, you see all the good in them, all the Christ in them. God sees Christ, His Son, in us and loves us. And so we should see Christ in others, *and nothing else*, and love them. There can never be enough of it," wrote Dorothy Day. "This is not easy. Everyone will try to kill that love in you."

She was right. If we soften toward those who hurt us or forgive too easily those who cheat us, the world labels us as losers, too trusting for our own good. Jesus tells us to trust anyway, forgive anyway, love anyway, always.

Meditation: Who is your enemy? Is it the person halfway around the world fighting an actual war, or is it the neighbor who makes life difficult, or the boss who is never satisfied? Enemies come in all shapes and sizes and forms, and sometimes they don't even look like "enemies." Can you start with one "enemy," one person who is difficult to love, and pour Christlike love into that relationship? Can you draw love out of a seemingly hopeless place this Lent?

Prayer: During this desert season, when we spend so much time looking inward and reflecting on our own spiritual struggles, help us, Jesus, to remember to look outward toward those who might be crying out for the healing touch of love and compassion. Give us the courage to love in the face of hate.

An Evolving Faith

Readings: Gen 15:5-12, 17-18; Phil 3:17–4:1; Luke 9:28b-36

Scripture:
"[O]ur citizenship is in heaven,
  and from it we also await a savior, the Lord Jesus Christ.
He will change our lowly body
  to conform with his glorified body." (Phil 3:20-21)

Reflection: For the longest time, the transfiguration eluded me. It was one of those scriptural references that was oh-so-familiar and oh-so-foreign at the same time. I could see the significance of the event in the lives of Peter, John, and James, but what did it have to do with my life in the here and now? Then, one morning as I sat in silence with these words, the confusion fell away and it all made sense.

When Jesus takes the three up to the mountain, it's meant to give them encouragement, an image to hold onto when times get hard. And it's meant to do the same for us. Today's readings try to drive home that point. Transfiguration abounds, and not just on Mount Tabor in the familiar gospel story. In Genesis, God tells Abraham that his descendants will be as numerous as the stars in the sky, and in the First Letter to the Philippians, Paul says God will "change our lowly body to conform with his glorified body." Again and again we are reminded that our faith is not meant to be static but ever-changing. We are called to be transfigured and transfiguring.

We may not shine like the sun on the outside, but when we turn our lives over to God, we, too, will be filled with a light that not only transforms us from the inside out but also transforms all those we meet with the spirit of Jesus Christ blazing in our hearts, in our words, in our actions.

The apostles were filled with fear at the sight of Jesus transfigured, and we may feel the same way when confronted with the radical shift required of a life lived in the light of Christ. But we have to remember the words spoken to the apostles then and to us today: "This is my chosen Son; listen to him."

Meditation: Try to imagine yourself on the mountain with Jesus today. Would it be enough to transfigure your heart and soul? How might you be transfigured if you let go of your fears and trusted in Jesus' promises?

Prayer: Today we pray for the patience and trust and willingness to listen in silence to what Jesus is trying to speak to our heart. We pray for the courage to hear his words, even if they are difficult, so that we might be transfigured and transformed.

Diamond in the Rough

Readings: 1 Pet 5:1-4; Matt 16:13-19

Scripture:
"And so I say to you, you are Peter,
and upon this rock I will build my Church." (Matt 16:18)

Reflection: Peter has always been one of my favorites, which accounts for the carved wooden rooster alongside the cross in our family room and the small plastic rooster peeking out from my sacred space in my basement office. Peter doubts, he denies, he runs away, and yet Jesus saw fit to call him the "rock" and to entrust his church to him. Every time I see one of my little roosters, I remember that Jesus doesn't call any of us because he wants perfect disciples; he calls us because he wants faithful disciples.

In today's gospel, Peter says what none of the others were even thinking: "You are the Christ, the Son of the living God." Even with that knowledge, which clearly came from heaven, Peter messes up again and again. Imagine for a moment that Jesus looks at you and says, "Get behind me, Satan." Peter asks Jesus to give him the ability to walk on water, and then begins to sink like a stone when doubt and fear creep in. I don't know about you, but I find tremendous comfort in all of that. If Jesus can see Peter's imperfections up close and still give him the keys to the kingdom, well, maybe there's some hope for me. Even while he is aware that denial is imminent, Jesus still puts his trust in Peter, because he knows that underneath all the flaws on the surface there beats the heart of a true disciple.

The first reading gives us a glimpse into the Peter Jesus must have recognized beneath the rough exterior: a fisherman with the heart of a shepherd, one who knew that people would be drawn to God not by force but by love, who urged others to bring people to Christ not through power but through example. If Jesus could see that potential in Peter, I wonder what he might see in me?

Meditation: Do you ever feel as though your mistakes and failings cut you off from God's mercy and love? Can you see yourself in Peter and learn to trust even when you want to run and hide? Can you, by your example, help others see their own belovedness in God's eyes?

Prayer: God of compassion, thank you for accepting us as we are, for loving us without conditions, without requirements. Help us to be faithful disciples, even if we are not perfect disciples.

February 23: Tuesday of the Second Week of Lent

Letting Go

Readings: Isa 1:10, 16-20; Matt 23:1-12

Scripture:
"Whoever exalts himself will be humbled;
   but whoever humbles himself will be exalted."
   (Matt 23:12)

Reflection: When I walked into the sacrament of reconciliation a few years back, I sat down and confessed that I felt like a hypocrite because I don't practice what I preach. Almost daily I blog about the spiritual journey and how to discover the divine in the everyday. I give retreats and workshops. I write books and columns. But, more often than not, I find myself wishing I could follow my own advice. I desperately want to do all the wonderful things I know will lead me toward God, but getting myself to clean up my spiritual act is more difficult than getting myself to clean up our disheveled basement. I want an easier way, but there is no easy way to God.

The priest in confession that day said, "You sound like a priest." With those words I felt my clenched jaw muscles slacken, not because that statement legitimized my feelings and actions (or inactions) but because it reminded me I am only human. We are all only human. We do what we can, but we can't do it perfectly. We understand with our heads what needs to be done, but, often, like the Pharisees in today's gospels, we get caught up in the exterior trappings and don't let the message sink down into our hearts where it needs to take root. We mistakenly begin to believe that the esteem of others or places of honor—wherever we seek "honor"—are more important than those unseen places deep within where the really important growth happens.

Rather than see our failures as hypocrisy, maybe we can see them as signs of dependence on God. We can't do this alone. We need to humble ourselves before God in order to get to the only place of honor that matters: heaven.

Meditation: Have you allowed yourself to get caught up in the external trappings of spirituality at the expense of your interior life? Today plan to loosen your grip on life and let God take the reins instead.

Prayer: Dear God, give us the humility to detach ourselves from the need to seek places of honor in this life and to search instead for the small, quiet places where you are hiding in plain sight. Help us to realize, finally, that our practice is far more powerful than our preaching.

Comfort and Courage

Readings: Jer 18:18-20; Matt 20:17-28

Scripture:
Jesus said in reply,
  "You do not know what you are asking.
Can you drink the chalice that I am going to drink?"
They said to him, "We can." (Matt 20:22)

Reflection: When I was a little girl, I would read stories of the saints before bed each night. I was fascinated by the courage of these holy people, some of them not much older than I was at the time, and I would imagine myself in their shoes. Would I have remained faithful in the face of doubt and questioning, suffering or death? My answer would always be, "Yes!" It was easy to take such a brave and noble position from the comfort of my soft bed with the blue and white comforter.

From the warmth of my grown-up bed today, my answer to that question is still a resounding "Yes!" but it's said with a little unease and a lot of fear. Although no one is threatening my life because of my faith in Jesus, others around the globe are not so fortunate. Persecution exists in far too many places. Men, women, and children are left with nothing but the clothes on their backs, their homes are ransacked, their churches are burned, their lives are threatened or, in some cases, snuffed out in terrifying ways.

In today's gospel, Jesus asks James and John if they can drink from the cup that he is going to drink, and, like children who don't fully understand the question, they answer with a resounding "Yes!" And they mean it, but soon they come to know just how difficult it will be to live up to that seemingly easy answer. For us today, even if our lives are not threatened, our faith may put us in tough spots—with friends, with family members, on public issues. Those are just tiny little sips from the cup. Others, people no different from us except for their geography, have been asked to drink fully. Would our "yes" be as quick or as easy if we had to trade places with them?

Meditation: Have you ever experienced any sort of "persecution" for your faith, even in a minimal way? How did you feel at that moment? Now imagine what it is like for those who suffer true persecution. How would your faith sustain you if all outward signs of your faith were taken away?

Prayer: Heavenly Father, today we pray for those who are persecuted for their faith. Give them comfort when they are afraid, give them courage when they are threatened, give them hope when they are despairing.

The Desert We Create

Readings: Jer 17:5-10; Luke 16:19-31

Scripture:
Cursed is the man who trusts in human beings,
   who seeks his strength in flesh,
      whose heart turns away from the Lord.
He is like a barren bush in the desert. (Jer 17:5-6)

Reflection: I love the scrubby, dry landscape of the Texas Hill Country. There's something powerful about its starkness. And yet, throughout the eight years I lived in Texas, I always missed the changing seasons of my home state of New York. The repeating cycle from lush summer lawns to dazzling autumn leaves to monochrome winter snow to bright spring regrowth sets life to a sacred rhythm. I guess that's why today's first reading from Jeremiah set me on edge. I couldn't get past the barren bush that "enjoys no change of season" as metaphor for those who trust humans more than God. Uh-oh. I almost wanted to turn around to see if maybe God was talking to someone standing behind me. No such luck.

I have issues with trust. Not with trusting other people, but with trusting God. I spend a lot of time in fear—fear of things that could happen to my children, fear of what might happen to me or my husband, fear of financial stuff, health stuff, professional stuff, every kind of "stuff" you can imagine. I expend lots of energy on fear, so much energy, in fact, that I probably am very much like that fried desert bush in Jeremiah that doesn't have the resources to enjoy the seasons.

I don't know about you, but I listen mostly to my own worried mind, thinking that somehow if I worry enough I can keep my problems at bay. But God challenges us to do just the opposite, to fall back into his arms and be caught by love. God will guide us out of our self-made deserts and into a lush land where we can finally enjoy all the sacred seasons of our lives.

Meditation: What deserts have you created for yourself? In what or whom do you place your trust? Do you find it hard to "let go and let God"? As you journey through the desert of Lent, begin to focus on those places in your daily life that need pruning, watering, maybe even outright uprooting.

Prayer: God of mercy, you ask only that we place our trust in you, but it is hard to let go of the worries and fears that crowd our thoughts and constrict our hearts. Help us to surrender it all to you, to give up the illusion of control and go from barren to bursting with new life.

An Unearned Inheritance

Readings: Gen 37:3-4, 12-13a, 17b-28a; Matt 21:33-43, 45-46

Scripture:
"Finally, he sent his son to them,
   thinking, 'They will respect my son.'
But when the tenants saw the son, they said to one another,
   'This is the heir.
Come, let us kill him and acquire his inheritance.'"
   (Matt 21:37-38)

Reflection: In one of his most famous books, *The Return of the Prodigal Son*, Henri Nouwen wrote, "Resentment and gratitude cannot coexist, since resentment blocks the perception and experience of life as a gift. My resentment tells me that I don't receive what I deserve. It always manifests itself in envy."

Today's first reading from Genesis and the gospel parable from Matthew are about the kind of resentment that not only turns gratitude into envy but love into hate. Somehow, when we focus only on our lack—like the brothers in the story of Joseph or the tenants in the parable about the vineyard—our common humanity falls victim to our personal agenda.

During this slow journey toward Jesus' crucifixion, we have today's allusions to Jesus' incarnation and our inability to gratefully and gracefully accept our own inheritance, even when it comes to us in the most dramatic fashion, a gift so great only faith can make sense of it.

"Finally, he sent his son to them, thinking, 'They will respect my son,'" we hear in the gospel parable, knowing full well that even as Jesus spoke the words others were plotting to arrest him and eventually kill him.

But we did not lose our inheritance, just the opposite. God sent us his Son not only as a messenger but as a Savior willing to die for our transgressions. It is amazing that in the face of that unconditional love and mercy we still manage to reject the cornerstone in both small and great ways in our daily life. Because we think we deserve better, more, most.

Even then, even when our selfishness blinds us to the gift in front of us, God does not lose faith in us, does not stop loving us, because we are his own.

Meditation: Gratitude transforms things, transforms us. It's no coincidence that gratitude journals have become wildly popular in so many different circles, from Catholic to New Age to secular self-help. Can you take note of at least three things for which you are grateful today?

Prayer: Son of God, you came to live among us, to live as one of us in order to bring about our eternal salvation, a gift we assuredly do not deserve. Today we give thanks for an inheritance we have not earned and often reject.

Flashes of Light

Readings: Mic 7:14-15, 18-20; Luke 15:1-3, 11-32

Scripture:
"My son, you are here with me always;
everything I have is yours.
But now we must celebrate and rejoice,
because your brother was dead and has come to life
again;
he was lost and has been found." (Luke 15:31-32)

Reflection: I have a friend who used to talk a lot about her "conversion experience." Although she had been baptized Catholic, she was not raised in the faith. A revert, she calls herself. When she talked about the way Jesus had come into her life with a force that could not be ignored, I felt a pang of jealousy. Sometimes she would say, "I'm sure you understand from your own conversion experience." And I would think to myself, "Where is my conversion moment? I've been here all along, God. I want my moment!"

Like the older son in today's gospel parable, I was frustrated and a little angry over what I felt was rightfully mine, not for anything exceptional I had done but simply for trying—and often failing—to do what was expected of me. But no one kills the fatted calf for lukewarm efforts, spiritual or otherwise. And yet, that doesn't mean that God hasn't been there for us in equal, or perhaps even greater, measure.

A few years ago, when I was part of a retreat team, I was asked to speak about grace. As I dug deeper into my relationship with Jesus, I realized that while I hadn't had any lightning bolt conversion moments, I had clearly witnessed countless flickers of light over the years—the death of my mother, the birth of my children, the loss of a job. God had given me small but steady doses of grace all along the way. I had just been too busy to notice how God had entered into my life during some of my most critical moments, conversion moments.

We do not need to be a lost cause in order to be found. We can be found day by day, if we enter into our relationship with God with the loyalty of the older son and the hunger of the younger son. When we approach God with passionate seeking over lukewarm obedience, we find that conversion moments are all around us.

Meditation: Have you ever had a lightning bolt conversion experience? How did it change you? If not, can you spot smaller conversion moments that have gone unnoticed but clearly helped guide you to where you are today?

Prayer: Abba, Father, you love all of your children—the lost and the found—with the same forgiving heart. Guide us home; give us wisdom; convert our hearts.

Reaching for the Sun

Readings: Exod 3:1-8a, 13-15; 1 Cor 10:1-6, 10-12; Luke 13:1-9

Scripture:
"He said to him in reply,
    'Sir, leave it for this year also,
    and I shall cultivate the ground around it and fertilize it;
    it may bear fruit in the future.
If not you can cut it down.'" (Luke 13:8-9)

Reflection: About ten years ago, when I was relandscaping our front yard, I had my heart set on a "Prairie Fire" crab apple tree. The blossoms were supposed to be more vibrant than typical varieties found in our upstate New York region. And so, for Mother's Day that year, my husband and children gave me a tree. I planted it in the perfect spot, but not long after, all the leaves fell off, and it looked so pitiful neighbors would comment as they passed by. The consensus was that this tree had to go, but I refused. I believed in this tree. I fertilized and pruned and hoped. Ten years later, that little tree proved me right when it pushed out a single pink bloom, securing its spot on our lawn forever.

Many of us are very much like that struggling crab apple tree, or, as in the case of today's gospel parable, the barren fig tree. From all outward appearances, we've squandered our resources, "exhausted the soil" of God's love. But God will not give up on us just yet. We are too precious in his sight, worth more time, more resources, more love. God patiently waits for us to bear fruit, even one single bright blossom as a sign of faith.

When we look at all of today's readings combined, it would be easy to get disheartened. In the first reading, we see Moses called by "I AM" and sent to save the Israelites. But by the second reading, St. Paul reminds us that those same Israelites were struck down in the desert, and we might experience the same if we remain barren by choosing evil over good. The fig tree hangs in the balance, waiting for us to decide its fate.

God keeps pouring resources down on us. Scripture and sacraments, mercy and compassion soak our roots, but do they course through our veins with purpose? Only then will we finally blossom into what God intended us to be.

Meditation: Are there areas of your life that need pruning? Where are you getting your nourishment? Do you give yourself time each day to bask in the light and life-giving waters of God's word?

Prayer: Creator God, help us to cultivate the seed of your love within our souls so that we may bear good fruit. Be patient with us, even when we waste your gifts and squander your love.

Finding Miracles in the Mundane

Readings: 2 Kgs 5:1-15ab; Luke 4:24-30

Scripture:
"My father," they said,
   "if the prophet had told you to do something extra-
      ordinary,
   would you not have done it?
All the more now, since he said to you,
   'Wash and be clean,' should you do as he said."
      (2 Kgs 5:13b)

Reflection: When I was on retreat a few years ago, Paulist Father Tom Ryan, who was leading the weekend, told us that living a more contemplative and prayerful life boiled down to taking "a loving look at the real." I was at once intrigued and ever-so-slightly annoyed because, let's face it, we often want the prescription for a better spiritual life to be something mystical, something extraordinary, something akin to what we imagine the saints must have experienced.

Like Naaman in today's first reading, we're put off by the suggestion that something so ordinary could cleanse us, heal us, transform us. And like the people in Jesus' hometown, we often can't accept that someone or something that has been right in front of us all along might hold the key to our ultimate salvation. You can almost imagine the people of

Nazareth talking amongst themselves. "Isn't that Joseph the carpenter's son? Who does he think he is?" It was hard for them to believe that their ordinary lives and ordinary town could produce someone so extraordinary.

Are we caught up in the same shortsightedness? Do we look at our real lives, the ebb and flow of normal joys and sorrows, and assume God couldn't or wouldn't show up there?

My retreat leader had a valid point. When we take "a loving look at the real," we begin to see God's hand at work amid the ordinariness of our lives. God is in the details, after all. Not only in the details of a Michelangelo masterpiece, not only in the details of the lives of well-known saints, but in the details of our lives right now, this minute. What do we see when we take a long loving look at the real?

Meditation: Where has God shown up in your life today? Do you often shrug off ordinary moments of grace, assuming they are too mundane or too "real" to mean anything of mystical proportions? What if you are no different from the saints and sages, save for the realization that holiness is all around you? Today, take a loving look at all that is real in your life.

Prayer: Dear Jesus, help us to recognize you in the details of daily life. Gives us eyes to see and ears to hear above the din of a world that tells us to doubt, to denigrate, to dismiss what is not extraordinary.

Mercy Sought, Mercy Given

Readings: Dan 3:25, 34-43; Matt 18:21-35

Scripture:
"Lord, if my brother sins against me,
how often must I forgive him?" (Matt 18:21b)

Reflection: My husband and I attended a Worldwide Marriage Encounter weekend a few years ago, and one of the many things that struck me as a true-but-difficult teaching was the instruction to not only say "I'm sorry" when I hurt my spouse but to ask, "Do you forgive me?" And, as a spouse, to be willing to say in return, "I forgive you," and really mean it.

There's a not-so-subtle difference between offering or accepting an apology and offering or accepting forgiveness. One is fairly easy to do because it comes from our head; the other comes from our heart and so it costs something, especially when we are the ones offering forgiveness. So often pride or resentment or insecurity get in the way of true forgiveness, but that only serves to reinforce the walls that divide us.

In today's gospel, Jesus reminds the disciples and us that we must be willing to forgive and forgive and forgive again, if we hope to receive the same from God. The parable shows us just how difficult a proposition that is. The servant knew how to beg for mercy for himself but not how to show mercy toward another. Do we, like him, expect forgiveness even when we are unwilling to give it?

I'm sure most of us can't possibly add up the number of times we've asked for this kind of reciprocal mercy in the words of the Our Father: "And forgive us our trespasses, / as we forgive those who trespass against us." We're telling God right up front that we would like to be forgiven in the same way we forgive. Sobering food for thought, isn't it? What if God forgave us as we forgive others?

Meditation: Why is it so hard to ask for forgiveness, and even harder to give it? What is keeping you from forgiving completely? Do you ask for mercy from God but withhold it from loved ones? If there is someone who needs your forgiveness, can you work toward being able to offer that gift with love before the end of the Lenten season?

Prayer: Merciful Father, we count on your willingness to forgive our sins no matter how many times we fall. Thank you for your boundless compassion. Soften our hearts so that we may know how to forgive those who have wronged us and finally let go of lingering anger, injury, and resentment.

Tough Love

Readings: Deut 4:1, 5-9; Matt 5:17-19

Scripture:
"[B]e earnestly on your guard
   not to forget the things which your own eyes have seen,
   nor let them slip from your memory as long as you live,
   but teach them to your children and to your children's
      children." (Deut 4:9b)

Reflection: From its earliest days, our faith was handed down through stories. The original disciples did not want to forget—could not forget—the things their own eyes had seen, and so they told and retold stories from the life of Jesus until finally someone wrote them down.

Many of us do the same with our own family histories. We tell our children about great-grandparents and grandparents who have died. We recall special moments from our childhoods, silly moments, difficult moments, stories filled with quirks and characters, laughter and tears.

Although today's readings have quite a bit of scare factor in them, there is always that element of love coursing through them, not completely unlike some of our own childhood stories. We may remember the times our parents laid down what seemed like strict rules and curfews even as they carted us off for a fun beach vacation. The discipline did not negate the love and joy. In hindsight, we can see the rules themselves were a sign of love. And so it is with today's readings.

In a world of moral relativism, it's easy to focus on Jesus as a good man who loved everyone. There's a tendency to acknowledge and accept his mercy but not his expectations. Yes, Jesus loves us—just like a caring parent—but Jesus challenges us as well. Heaven comes at a price.

Can we see the commandments not as restraints but as gifts, not as hindrances but as wings? Do we recognize the rules as a sign of love, a path designed to take us where we need to go in the happiest and holiest fashion? Our world tries to tell us we are free to do what we want, but we need to be on guard, to remember the stories of faith that lead to real freedom, inner freedom.

Meditation: Do you remember a time from childhood when what seemed like unnecessary harshness on the part of your parents turned out to be exactly what you needed? What stories from our faith stand out as the ones that best demonstrate God's love for you?

Prayer: Merciful God, forgive us for being like unruly children at times, demanding gifts but unwilling to do what is required of us. Give us the humility to step back and let you lead, to recognize the signs of your love in the stories of our faith.

Putting Poetry into Practice

Readings: Jer 7:23-28; Luke 11:14-23

Scripture:
This is what I commanded my people:
  Listen to my voice;
  then I will be your God and you shall be my people.
    (Jer 7:23a)

Reflection: St. Benedict of Nursia begins his Rule with the words, "Listen with the ear of your heart." That line is not only poetic but practical, at least spiritually speaking. We can listen without ever hearing a word. We can pray without ever being truly present. We can profess without ever putting beliefs into practice. Without love, without committing our heart, we are, as St. Paul said, just clashing cymbals.

In today's first reading Jeremiah tells us that God wanted nothing more than for people to listen, to walk in his ways, but they turned their backs and "stiffened their necks." In the gospel, Jesus, too, warns against what may happen if we do not keep up our strength through prayer and practice. We may not be strong enough to fight off the forces of evil clawing at our spiritual doorstep. "Whoever is not with me is against me, and whoever does not gather with me scatters," he says (Luke 11:23).

All of that begins with listening, because that is where the Spirit speaks, that is where we gather, that is where we strengthen our souls against temptation. How can we hear the Spirit whispering over the constant and clanging noise of the world around us? By cultivating silence in our lives, even if only a few minutes each day.

"Accepting silence is the first step toward intimacy with God," writes Norvene Vest in *No Moment Too Small: Rhythms of Silence, Prayer & Holy Reading*. "Silence creates an environment in which God can be heard and welcomed."

Today, right now, let's turn off everything around us that makes noise, close our door, turn out the lights, close our eyes, and listen with the ear of our heart.

Meditation: Can you build five minutes of silence into your daily routine? Do you find silence scary or soothing, unnerving or calming? What is it about silence that makes you uncomfortable? After one week of daily silent prayer, see if you notice a difference, a deepening, in your connection to God and your relationship with others.

Prayer: Holy Spirit, speak to us in the silence. Slow down the thoughts churning in the background of our minds so that we can hear God's word above our own internal chaos. Allow this silent prayer to take root in our heart and soul and move outward, like a wave of peace embracing everyone we meet.

Perfectly Imperfect

Readings: Hos 14:2-10; Mark 12:28-34

Scripture:
"You shall love your neighbor as yourself." (Mark 12:31)

Reflection: When I was writing my book *Cravings: A Catholic Wrestles with Food, Self-Image, and God*, I spent a lot of time thinking about Jesus' admonition to "love your neighbor as yourself." As someone who has struggled mightily for the better part of a lifetime to see myself as lovable, it wasn't good news for my neighbors. If I treated or spoke to others the way I treat and speak to myself, someone probably would have duct taped my mouth shut by now.

Many of us were raised to believe true humility meant thinking less of ourselves. We were taught to see love of self as vain or sinful, but the reality is that if we can't love ourselves at least a little, it becomes very hard to love anyone else. The perfection we expect of ourselves, which seems noble and self-effacing, often translates into the impossibly high standards we set for the people around us.

We create self-made parameters for what we think will make us worthy of love. I will be loveable when I . . . lose ten pounds, get a better job, quit smoking, start exercising. We cut God out of the loop and appoint ourselves judge and jury. We think we're being virtuous by being so hard on ourselves, but in reality, we're just practicing an upside down sort of narcissism, pouring all our energy into trying to perfect ourselves instead of pouring all our energy into trying to perfect our relationship with God.

Today's gospel reminds us that only when we learn to love God with all our heart and soul and mind and strength can we begin to reflect that love inwardly toward ourselves and outwardly toward our neighbor.

We are called to love as God loves, even if we can't come close to perfection. We can try. Starting today. Starting with ourselves.

Meditation: Do you have a hard time seeing yourself as loved and loving yourself as you are? When you reflect on your relationships, do you see places where that lack of self-love translates as a lack of compassion for others? Love of neighbor begins within each of our hearts.

Prayer: God of compassion, lead us to a place of self-acceptance so that we may better love you and our neighbors. Open our eyes to the goodness around us and help us to become a conduit for your love.

Prayer Essentials

Readings: Hos 6:1-6; Luke 18:9-14

Scripture:
"But the tax collector stood off at a distance
   and would not even raise his eyes to heaven
   but beat his breast and prayed,
   'O God, be merciful to me a sinner.'" (Luke 18:13)

Reflection: For a long time, I had an hourly chime on my office computer. It was a long, low ringing, like the sound of a Tibetan singing bowl being struck with a wooden mallet. I originally installed the chime as part of an effort to be more mindful about my day. I would get so caught up in my work and email and online conversations that it was easy to lose sight of the peaceful center around which I so desperately wanted my life to revolve.

I quickly developed a little prayer routine to go along with the hourly chime. Every time it started to ring, I would begin saying the Jesus Prayer: "Lord Jesus Christ, Son of God, have mercy on me, a sinner." Over and over I would say it until the last reverberations ended. At first it seemed insignificant, but before long I realized that those few seconds of silent prayer at the top of every hour were starting to transform my day, and my heart along with it.

As soon as I heard the little "thunk" sound that always preceded the ringing, I would feel my shoulders relax. My back would straighten, my eyes close, and my breathing slow. In those ten or fifteen seconds, I would be called back to the most essential elements of our faith: Jesus is my Lord and the Son of God. He is merciful. I am a sinner.

That one-line prayer, so similar to the words of the tax collector in today's gospel, says so much. When we are humble enough to accept our sinfulness and seek forgiveness, God's mercy washes over us like rain over parched earth.

Meditation: Your logical self may want to tally up all the things you've done right in this life to comfort yourself with visions of heaven in the hereafter, but today you are reminded that you can only enter heaven if you acknowledge a tally of a different sort—your sinfulness. Are you willing to humble yourself before God and ask for healing? Can you develop a ritual that calls you back to this place at least a few times each day so that God's mercy can transform you from the inside out?

Prayer: Merciful Lord, we stand before you all too aware of our sinfulness. Have mercy on us, as you did the tax collector, and guide us gently home.

A Dance of Faith

Readings: Josh 5:9a, 10-12; 2 Cor 5:17-21; Luke 15:1-3, 11-32

Scripture:
Whoever is in Christ is a new creation:
the old things have passed away;
behold, new things have come. (2 Cor 5:17)

Reflection: So often I have wanted to become "a new creation," thinking all my problems would be solved and life would be so much easier, if only I could be transformed all at once and for all time. But today's readings—Paul's letter to the Corinthians and the gospel story of the Prodigal Son—remind us that becoming a new creation is a process. Even if we are reborn in Christ, we may find ourselves straying far from home like the Prodigal Son and needing to return again and again for forgiveness and reconciliation.

In her book *Wayfaring: A Gospel Journey in Everyday Life*, Margaret Silf writes that true transformation requires "radical realignment in our lives." "A decisive act of will is required to turn away from those things that are entangling us further and further into untruth, deception, and delusion, and to turn in the direction of what we know, deep in the core of our being, is true," she says. "The story of the Prodigal Son illustrates just how hard this turnaround can be. This is not a once-and-for-all 'conversion' experience, crucial though such an experience may have been in our lives. It is a 'turning' (or 'metanoia') that may be asked of us many times a day in our ordinary lived experience."

If we accept that we cannot make this transformation on our own and that it will be an ongoing dance of two steps forward, one step back, becoming a new creation suddenly seems less foreboding and more realistic. We can become a new creation today, and, if we slip, we can start over again tomorrow. Like the loving father in the story of the Prodigal Son, God will be there waiting to celebrate with us every time.

Meditation: What difficult truth about yourself do you know deep in the core of being that you have never spoken aloud? If you were to unleash that truth or face that truth, would you move one step closer to becoming a "new creation"? What would you look like if you became the new creation you believe God made you to be?

Prayer: Beloved Father, we thank you for waiting patiently for us when we wander far from your side and for rejoicing in our return every time we come running back to you. Help us to become new creations, reborn through reconciliation and love.

Faith Beyond Reason

Readings: Isa 65:17-21; John 4:43-54

Scripture:
"Unless you people see signs and wonders, you will not
believe." (John 4:48)

Reflection: Taking things on faith isn't an easy proposition,
at least not in our show-me-the-money society. "You have
to see it to believe it," we're told. "You're *never* going to
believe this," we say.

How would we have fared had we lived in the time and
place of Jesus during his ministry? Even those who saw
miracles occur right before their eyes, whose own children
or servants or selves were healed, often without anything
more than Jesus' verbal promise, struggled to believe. Jesus
defied reason and logic, rules and the status quo.

On the flip side, of course, were those who believed even
without seeing, those who knew in their hearts that Jesus
was the Messiah, the Christ. They did not need a miracle.
They did not need to taste water turned to wine. They did
not need to see a servant cured, a man raised. They simply
knew without question, even when knowing defied
reason.

Although we may not take much on faith in our day-to-
day practical lives, we take an awful lot on faith where it

counts: in our bound-for-eternity spiritual lives. While some of us may be blessed with miraculous moments of our own, firsthand "proof" that there is more to come, most of us believe without seeing, follow without knowing where we will land.

That faith is a miracle in itself, when we stop to think about it. Why do we have this gift of faith when others don't? What keeps us faithful day after day, year after year, sometimes during incredibly difficult times that put us to the test? That kind of faith is not our own doing. That kind of faith is a gift, a miracle. Maybe it's the sign we've been seeking all this time.

Meditation: If you had seen Jesus perform miraculous signs before your eyes, would your faith be deeper than it is now, or do you believe deeply and fervently, even without seeing? Do you often pray for "a sign" to shore up your faith? Are you missing smaller signs that remind you of God's presence all along life's way?

Prayer: Dear Jesus, we desperately want to believe without needing signs and wonders, but we are human, and sometimes we stumble and doubt. Help our unbelief. Let us feel your presence in our lives, especially when we are faltering. Give us faith that never wavers.

March 8: Tuesday of the Fourth Week of Lent

Getting Unstuck

Readings: Ezek 47:1-9, 12; John 5:1-16

Scripture:
"Do you want to be well?" (John 5:6b)

Reflection: Most of us know what we need to do to be healthier, happier, more peaceful, and less stressed, but getting ourselves to do those things is another story. I'm a great one for coming up with lists: healthy recipes, spiritual reading, exercise plans, career goals. My problem is translating those lists into reality. More often than not, it doesn't happen. When I get busy and stressed, exercise, prayer time, and healthy diet are the first things to go. But that's just the opposite of how we should operate.

St. Francis de Sales said, "Half an hour's meditation each day is essential, except when you are busy. Then a full hour is needed."

Too often we think of the things that make us "well"—prayer being at the top of that list—as luxuries, things we get to enjoy only after everything on our "to do" list is complete. But Jesus, in today's gospel, reminds us that to get well we need to listen to his instructions and then, in the words of the old Nike commercial, "just do it."

Many of us get stuck—physically, mentally, emotionally, spiritually—in the same place for years. We watch other people passing us by, enjoying the healing waters we thirst for day after day. What is it that is crippling us? Is it a physical ailment like the man in today's gospel, or is it an addiction of some sort, to food or alcohol, shopping or social media? Is it fear and doubt, or pride and vanity? What is the "mat" to which we cling like a life preserver? Only when we are willing to pick it up, throw it off, and walk forward in trust, will we finally be well, body and soul.

Meditation: Look at the many aspects of your life. What changes could help you become "well"? What about your prayer life? Do you cut back when life gets busy or stressful? Can you begin to trust that the time you spend in prayer will smooth out the stresses rather than add to them?

Prayer: Healing Lord, we know if we trust in your word, we can throw off anything that holds us back and walk without fear into a life where blessings abound, even when we struggle. Give us the courage to pick up our mats and follow you.

Unforgettable and Unforgotten

Readings: Isa 49:8-15; John 5:17-30

Scripture:
Can a mother forget her infant,
    be without tenderness for the child of her womb?
Even should she forget,
    I will never forget you. (Isa 49:15)

Reflection: When my oldest child, Noah, was eighteen months old, my husband and I learned I was pregnant with our second child, and we were ecstatic. But only a few weeks into my pregnancy, long before I'd seen my baby on ultrasound, my mother's intuition told me something was very wrong. Just as I could sense when Noah was struggling with something in the next room, I could sense that my unborn baby was in trouble in my womb. And I was right. My baby, the one I call Grace, died before I finished my first trimester, but her presence is etched on my soul. Every August, when the date of my miscarriage rolls around, and in late February as her due date nears, I grieve for her again. I will never forget her, could never forget her.

So when I hear today's first reading from Isaiah, my mind rushes back to Grace and my other three babies. "Can a mother forget her infant, / be without tenderness for the child of her womb? / Even should she forget, / I will never forget you." Imagine God loving each one of us with a mother's love, with a force more powerful than sorrow or grief or death. And then in the gospel, we get the other half of the equation: God loving Jesus—and us by extension—with a father's love, if only we could accept his teachings, believe his words.

When my youngest, Chiara, was only three years old, she asked where she was before she was born, and then in answer to her own question, she said, "In God's dreams?" Yes, in God's dreams, in God's womb—beloved from before the beginning of time and unforgotten till the end.

Meditation: How blessed and lucky are we to have a God who is both mother and father to us, who loves us with a tenderness and fierceness beyond anything we can imagine? In your mind's eye, see yourself held in God's womb for all eternity. How does that feel? Can you carry that image forward to this moment and see how that love can shape this day, this Lent, this life?

Prayer: God of tenderness, we thank you for pouring your love out on us day after day, even when we aren't paying attention, even when we think we've been forgotten. Keep us safe in your palm until we return home to you.

Taking Off Our Masks

Readings: Exod 32:7-14; John 5:31-47

Scripture:
"They have soon turned aside from the way I pointed out
    to them,
    making for themselves a molten calf and worshiping it,
    sacrificing to it and crying out,
    'This is your God, O Israel,
    who brought you out of the land of Egypt!'" (Exod 32:8)

Reflection: Let's be honest. There is no getting around today's Scripture readings without a little tough love. I mean,
we've got God the Father ready to smite people in the first
reading from Exodus, if not for a little fast talking—and
pleading—on the part of Moses. And Jesus is showing more
than a little frustration with unbelievers in today's gospel
from John. Clearly people were getting on his last nerve,
which I totally understand as my beloved children come in
and interrupt me again and again while I write this piece. I
don't love them any less when I tell them they'd better listen
to me, or else. And that's basically what Jesus is telling us.
Pay attention. Or else.

We need tough love, don't we? As Moses begs God to have
mercy on his people, even as they bow down before a golden
calf of their own making, it would be oh-so-easy to think we

are safe from smiting because we would never make a golden calf. We are much more evolved than that, aren't we? Not so fast. Perhaps we've done just that but in a much less obvious form.

"We dismiss the golden calf story and its lessons at our peril," writes Elizabeth Scalia in her book *Strange Gods*. "It's true that we are no longer literally flinging our precious metals into a crucible and buffing up stolid beasts of burden to worship. In some ways matters are worse, for we do not know the idols we bow down to."

Idols are all around us, almost inescapable in our have-it-all world. Money, power, possessions are the obvious idols, but there are plenty of others lurking right out in the open: social media and other technology, sex, ideologies, physical fitness, anything that becomes so central to our life that it gets in the way of our relationship with God and colors our relationships with others.

Meditation: What are the idols in your life today? Is it something obvious or something that's easy to ignore? Sometimes we can mask our idols and pretend they are actually positives. What in your life today needs to be unmasked?

Prayer: Lord, God, we want nothing to come before you. We want nothing to come between us. Give us the clarity, honesty, and wisdom we need to rid ourselves of the idols we've created in place of you.

Fair-Weather Faith

Readings: Wis 2:1a, 12-22; John 7:1-2, 10, 25-30

Scripture:
"He professes to have knowledge of God
    and styles himself a child of the LORD.
To us he is the censure of our thoughts;
    merely to see him is a hardship for us." (Wis 2:13-14)

Reflection: My youngest daughter Chiara was a huge fan of a popular boy band for a while. She had posters and stickers of them all over her bedroom and a life-size cardboard cutout of her favorite. She couldn't get enough of them. And then, only a few months later, she declared the fascination over. She removed every sticker and poster. She had us put six-foot cardboard Louis out on the curb for trash pick-up. She threw away her fan calendar even though there were four months left in the year. Over. Done. Just seeing them created some sort of hardship for her.

We humans are fickle. We are easily bored, lured away, frustrated, and fearful. We become fans, groupies, followers, and then just as quickly we find a new obsession when being a fan loses its appeal or, even worse, becomes difficult. In today's readings, we see that fickleness playing out in frightening fashion. People who couldn't get enough of Jesus are suddenly ready to put him out on the curb, to have him arrested, to put him to death. Why? Because what he had to say was difficult to hear and even harder to accept. Rather than change their lives, the majority sought to end his.

We see the foreshadowing in Wisdom: "Let us beset the just one, because he is obnoxious to us; / he sets himself against our doings / . . . With revilement and torture let us put him to the test."

Despite the growing hostility, however, a band of true believers remained faithful. They had seen and heard enough to know that Jesus was the Messiah, even if that belief might bring them hardship. Where do we fall on the spectrum? Are we fickle when it comes to our faith, or do we remain steadfast even when it requires us to make difficult changes and choices?

Meditation: Have there been times in your life when you've been "gung ho" about your faith because of some superficial reason – a favorite pastor, a better music ministry, a pretty church? What happened when that reason disappeared? Did you start searching elsewhere for something to fill the void? How can you learn to be less fickle in your faith?

Prayer: Dear Jesus, we want to be true to you, even when the winds of change tempt us to look elsewhere for fulfillment. We want to grow in faith and love, even if it means facing challenges that make us uneasy.

Stories that Speak

Readings: Jer 11:18-20; John 7:40-53

Scripture:
"Never before has anyone spoken like this man."
  (John 7:46)

Reflection: As a writer, I am intimately aware of the power of words to reach people in deep, sometimes transforming ways. Not that I am necessarily able to do that with my own words, but I can recognize the gift in others—a story that makes me cry, an image that resonates deep within my soul, a turn of phrase that speaks to my heart. A good storyteller can make us feel as if his or her words were written just for us, a personal message meant to pull us out of our complacency and propel us forward with renewed joy, enthusiasm, hope, or compassion.

In today's gospel, the guards tell the Pharisees they did not arrest Jesus because "[n]ever before has anyone spoken like this man" (John 7:46). Even as nonbelievers, something about Jesus' words moved them, struck at their core. You can almost sense their awe.

Teaching through parables allowed Jesus to touch people's lives in ways that were easy to understand and difficult to ignore. In fields, on mountains, at the sea, in the temple, his words both delighted and disturbed people, and whispered to them in the silence of their hearts.

How do those same stories resonate with us today? Are we moved to quiet awe by what we hear? Maybe we don't always recognize the practical meanings behind the parables, the reasons fig trees and mustard seeds, yeast and new wine find their way into stories about salvation, but on a deeper level we connect. Even all these centuries later, feasts and famines, celebrations and sickness, scarcity and abundance, light and dark, life and death are woven into the fabric of our lives in both big and small ways.

"Never before has anyone spoken like this man." In breaking open the Word, we allow Jesus to break open our hearts and rewrite our own stories.

Meditation: Think of the parables and teachings of Jesus that resonate with you most deeply. Is there one story in particular that makes you feel the way the guards in today's gospel did, awed by Jesus' ability to speak to you in ways that no one and nothing else can?

Prayer: Dear Jesus, your words comfort us, challenge us, guide us, heal us. Never let us lose sight of the ways Scripture can transform our hearts and our lives.

Second Chances

Readings: Isa 43:16-21; Phil 3:8-14; John 8:1-11

Scripture:
> "Let the one among you who is without sin
> be the first to throw a stone at her." (John 8:7b)

Reflection: The popular 1970s TV movie *Jesus of Nazareth* has always been one of my all-time favorites, and today's gospel makes me flash back to the same scene played out on screen. The woman caught in adultery cowers in fear and shame. Her accusers taunt and threaten, as they gently bounce rocks in their hands, waiting for Jesus to say the word, "go." But Jesus says nothing. He sits on the ground and writes or "doodles" in the dirt. What exactly was he writing? Was it a message lost over time? In that moment, Jesus bends the angry mob's line in the sand into a new kind of truth, a circle that encompassed all of them, and all of us.

Even after the crowd moves on, the woman still cowers, waiting for the punishment she assumes must be coming, maybe not in the form of a rock but surely something that will hurt in some fashion. "'Has no one condemned you?' She replied, 'No one, sir.' Then Jesus said, 'Neither do I condemn you. Go, and from now on do not sin any more'" (John 8:10-11).

What must the woman have felt at that moment? Relief, yes, but perhaps something even bigger—absolute forgiveness and a second chance. It was a far cry from the painful death she was expecting.

God does not condemn us. We condemn ourselves. We condemn each other, not only by the sins we commit but by the sins we hold bound in those around us. The line in the sand of our souls can cut us off from God when we imagine we are not good enough to cross it, when we try to keep others in that dry, desperate place with us. But we can never be separated from God, not even by sins that make us cower in fear and shame.

Meditation: Is there something in your life that is keeping you from fully embracing God's mercy and love? Are you condemning yourself or someone else for a past sin? Can you drop the stones of anger, resentment, self-righteousness, or fear and accept that forgiveness is for you, for everyone?

Prayer: Jesus, we know the pain that comes from a sin we feel we can't escape. Soften our hearts today so that we may forgive ourselves, forgive others, and embrace the second chance you offer to those who are truly sorry.

Shadow Side

Readings: Dan 13:1-9, 15-17, 19-30, 33-62 or 13:41c-62; John 8:12-20

Scripture:
"I am the light of the world.
Whoever follows me will not walk in darkness,
    but will have the light of life." (John 8:12b)

Reflection: My youngest child, Chiara, is still afraid of the dark, despite the fact that she's ten years old and incredibly independent, brave, feisty, and fun. Every night when she goes to bed, she likes the door open, at least a crack, and the hall light on. After she's asleep, we swap the hall light for the bathroom nightlight, but always there is something to guide her should she find herself disoriented or downright scared. Even as grown-ups, there's something comforting about a light, no matter how small, glowing in the darkness. It gives us comfort. It gives us hope. It makes us feel a little less alone.

Today, in a gospel that focuses mostly on the dark and foreboding tensions between Jesus and the Pharisees, there is a glimmer of light to keep us going. "I am the light of the world. Whoever follows me will not walk in darkness, but will have the light of life," Jesus says.

Most of us are all too familiar with darkness. Every time struggles crop up in marriage, parenting, friendships, work, darkness rears its head, offering the false comfort of numbness or the life-sucking blackness of despair. But the Light is always there. The only real danger is when we stop looking.

Jesuit Father Walter Ciszek, who spent twenty-three years in a Siberian prison, wrote that his greatest despair was the "one moment of blackness" when he lost faith in God. "I had stood alone in a void and I had not even thought of or recalled the one thing that had been my constant guide, my only source of consolation in all other failures, my ultimate recourse: I had lost the sight of God," he wrote in *He Leadeth Me*.

We need not fear the dark; the Light is always shining for us.

Meditation: Have there been moments in your life when you lost sight of God? How did you eventually rediscover the light in your life? Today, focus on the light that shines daily into your life, even when it is at its darkest, even when it seems easier to settle into the blackness of fear and despair.

Prayer: God of light, your love burns through even the deepest fog and darkest shadows that cloud our vision. Focus our hearts on the Light of Christ that turns despair into hope, fear into joy, worry into trust.

Gratitude Attitude

Readings: Num 21:4-9; John 8:21-30

Scripture:
[W]ith their patience worn out by the journey,
the people complained against God and Moses.
    (Num 21:4-5)

Reflection: I hate to say it, but, boy, do I hear myself in the children of Israel as they wander the desert, tired and thirsty and "disgusted" with the wretched food. You don't have to put me in a desert and deny me dinner to get me to that point. I'm usually ready to complain at a moment's notice. Delayed plane: Why God? Child home with a cold on a day I have an important work appointment: Why God? Computer crash: Why God? You name it and I'll complain to God about it. It's amazing God takes any of my calls at this point.

When we first hear God's reaction to the Israelites' complaints—the snakebites and death—we might think, wow, harsh. But as soon as complaining turns to prayer, the landscape shifts and things take a turn for the better. That doesn't mean if we stop complaining and start praying about our delayed flight it will swoop us off to our destination on time, but if we can just step back for a minute and take in the bigger picture, it does shift our landscape as well. In the light of prayer and even gratitude for what we do have, we suddenly find patience and calm in the midst of what we don't have. It's a matter of perspective, really.

I don't think God expects us to take all things, even suffering, with a smile. Time and again, Jesus reminds us that we need to be persistent, perhaps even a little bit of a nag when we come to God in prayer. But there is a difference between angry annoyance and pleading prayer. One pushes God away; the other draws God near. The approach is up to us.

Meditation: Do you pray to God for help, or rail against God in anger when you are confused or desperate? Can you approach even difficult situations in your life with gratitude for what you have, not complaint for what you don't have? Can you look toward the signs of God present in your life and be saved?

Prayer: Father in heaven, you know how often we come to you, like a child clinging to the leg of a weary parent, looking for something, anything to make us feel better. Give us the strength to stop latching onto all the wrong things and to embrace all that is good in our lives right now.

Unfiltered Faith

Readings: Dan 3:14-20, 91-92, 95; John 8:31-42

Scripture:
"[Y]ou will know the truth, and the truth will set you free." (John 8:32)

Reflection: In our fiercely independent culture, "freedom" comes with a laundry list of expectations. It means we can do what we want, when we want. If something makes us unhappy, we can change it—move, quit, start over. We cling to our right to reinvent ourselves with the fierceness of a mama bear protecting her cub. But Jesus comes at that word from a very different place. In today's gospel, Jesus makes it clear that all the things that worldly freedom promises us can ensnare us and enslave us instead.

What does freedom look like if we strip it of its exterior trappings? If we didn't need to keep up with the Joneses—financially, socially, spiritually—what would we do differently? Would we give up the high-powered job that provides us with lots of extra money but robs us of family time? Would we stop spending our precious free time on TV shows and social media and start doing things that might actually feed our hearts and souls? Would we worry less about leasing the latest model car and instead finally own our faith in a deep and lasting way?

The people in the gospel story didn't really understand what Jesus is saying to them, and most of us today are probably listening with the same sorts of filters that color and distort his message. The truth can be uncomfortable and difficult, at least if we're honest about it. What is our truth and where is it taking us? If our lives are lived in the shadow of worldly needs and desires, there's a good chance it's not the kind of truth that frees us. Only Jesus can give us that, with a truth that can't be bought and sold. This truth must be earned the hard way.

Meditation: Look at your life, your truth. Have you created a "freedom" that holds you down or one that lifts you up? Is there one thing you can change that would bring you one step closer to the kind of truth that Jesus offers? Are you willing to make that change today?

Prayer: Jesus, you are the Way, the Truth, and the Life. Help us to keep our hearts and minds focused on that promise when the world tries to convince us there is a better way, an easier way. You are the only way. Only you can set our souls free.

Choosing Sides

Readings: Gen 17:3-9; John 8:51-59

Scripture:
"Amen, amen, I say to you,
  before Abraham came to be, I AM." (John 8:58)

Reflection: When I was writing *The Complete Idiot's Guide to the Catholic Catechism* a few years ago, there was one particular change required in order for the book to receive its *imprimatur*. It was such a seemingly simple change and yet so difficult to comprehend with our human minds. In the chapter on the Trinity, I had written that the Father, Son, and Spirit had existed since the beginning of time. My censor kindly reminded me that, no, the Trinity existed since *before* time began.

Although we know and believe the three Persons of the Trinity are one, it's easy to compartmentalize, to see God as Creator of all, including time itself, and Jesus and the Spirit as later additions. But our faith tells us that all are one from all time, that Father, Son, and Spirit brought this world into being together, as one. In today's gospel Jesus reminds us of that again.

The Jews question how Jesus could possibly know Abraham, and Jesus says, "Amen, amen, I say to you, before Abraham came to be, I AM." With that they wanted to stone him. It was a radical thing to hear then; it is a radical thing to hear now. In John's gospel today, and throughout this week of Lent, Jesus tries to drive home this point: He comes from the Father. He knows the Father. The Father sent him. They are one and the same. The gospel tells us that because of what he said, some came to believe in him, but even more turned on him.

Into which camp do we fall? Although we may profess it with our mouths week after week, day after day, do we believe it with our hearts and souls? Jesus is the Christ, the Son of the living God, the Word among us. He knew us before time began and loved us into being.

Meditation: The words I AM were spiritually charged for the Jewish people two thousand years ago, and they should be just as spiritually charged for us today. What do those words mean to you when you hear Jesus speak them?

Prayer: Jesus, Son of God, we profess our belief in you so often that sometimes we take it for granted. Help us to hear your words anew, to hold them in the silence of our hearts and allow them to transform us. "Lord, I believe. Help my unbelief."

Defining Jesus

Readings: Jer 20:10-13; John 10:31-42

Scripture:
"We are not stoning you for a good work but for
    blasphemy.
You, a man, are making yourself God." (John 10:33b)

Reflection: The reality of the incarnation is hard to fully comprehend or explain, even for those of us who believe deeply and unwaveringly. "Effing the ineffable," is how one theologian put it to me. Understanding how Jesus is both fully human and fully divine is, as Catholics will often say, "a mystery."

My husband and I decided to ask the students in our ninth-grade faith formation class to write down—anonymously— one thing they know or believe about Jesus. I knew we might be opening a can of worms. For many of these children, at least those who do not attend Mass regularly and come to faith formation mainly to get the sacraments, the thought of Jesus being both God and man might be as much of a shock to them as it was to the Jews of Jesus' time.

The answers we got back from our students fell just about everywhere on the faith spectrum. One did write, "Jesus is God." Others said that he was born of the Virgin Mary, died on a cross for our sins, and performed miracles. And one said, "I don't believe in Jesus, but, if he is real, then he helped people." And so we knew that one student in our group was bold enough to admit to her (or his) religion teachers that she (or he) didn't believe in Jesus, and yet was willing to leave the door open just a crack with that all-important "but . . ."

We will not be able to convince this student of the incarnation through words alone. After all, as we read in today's gospel, Jesus wasn't able to do that even through good works performed right before people's eyes. We have to draw people to Jesus by letting them see how our actions and our lives are transformed by knowing him, loving him. If people witness us living the Gospel with joy, they will want what we have and will gladly open wide the door to their hearts and say, "Yes, Lord, we believe."

Meditation: Who is Jesus to you? Do you tend to focus mainly on Jesus' divinity or his humanity? Today try to shift your focus and see *all* of Jesus.

Prayer: Christ our Savior, we thank you for coming down from heaven to live as one of us in order to save us. Help us draw others to you through the example of our lives.

Faith without Fanfare

Readings: 2 Sam 7:4-5a, 12-14a, 16; Rom 4:13, 16-18, 22; Matt 1:16, 18-21, 24a or Luke 2:41-51a

Scripture:
When Joseph awoke,
   he did as the angel of the Lord had commanded him
   and took his wife into his home. (Matt 1:24)

Reflection: Quiet strength and hidden holiness—those are the words that come to mind when I think of St. Joseph, who was so critical to our salvation story and yet so inconspicuous throughout Scripture. Save for a few well-known passages from the events surrounding the birth of Jesus and a few short but significant scenes from Jesus' infancy and early childhood, we know very little about Joseph. But what we do know speaks volumes. From those few stories we are able to piece together a powerful image of faith, determination, and love. Joseph quietly and courageously did what needed to be done to follow God's plan.

   Even before the angel appeared to him in a dream, saying, "Do not be afraid," we are told that Joseph was a "righteous man," unwilling to expose Mary to anymore hardship than she already faced. From that one passage alone, we can recognize a man of compassion, a man of justice, a man of God.

We can only assume that those qualities came into play later as he helped Mary raise Jesus. He would have taught Jesus not only how to be a skilled carpenter but also how to be a faithful Jewish man. Without fanfare and accolades or anecdotes, Joseph's character comes shining through. No wonder he is so beloved among our communion of saints. In Joseph's understated but unshakable faith, we catch a glimpse of what we have the potential to become. We don't need to make holy headlines. We just need to live out the story God has written for us, line by line, even if no one takes note of the details.

Meditation: Contemplate the scene from today's gospel. Imagine yourself in Joseph's shoes, feeling wronged over this child that is not yours, feeling confused about what to do next, feeling sad for this woman who was to be your bride. Now imagine you receive a message in a dream. Would you be able to follow the angel's instructions or would you be too caught up in the specifics of the circumstances to imagine a greater good playing out?

Prayer: Beloved St. Joseph, we turn to you today to seek your intercession for all those intentions we hold in the silence of our hearts but which we speak aloud to you today. Teach us to follow your example of quiet strength when circumstances shake our faith.

Into the Deep

Readings: Luke 19:28-40; Isa 50:4-7; Phil 2:6-11; Luke 22:14–23:56

Scripture:
[A]s he was approaching the slope of the Mount of
    Olives,
the whole multitude of his disciples
began to praise God aloud with joy
for all the mighty deeds they had seen. (Luke 19:36b)

Reflection: Although we have just officially entered Holy Week with great fanfare and the waving of palm branches, it is almost impossible from this vantage point not to fast-forward to what we know is coming in just a few days. We have been down this road before, and the reading of the Lord's passion lays it bare, a stark reminder of the suffering that culminated in Calvary, pushing humanity—then and now—toward a decision. Do we stand with Jesus, even under the weight of the cross, even under the threat of danger, maybe even death? Or do we run, maybe even betray?

The hour is coming. Quickly. Jesus knows it. The disciples can sense it, even if they are not completely aware of how brutal it will be. Fear is in the air, as the Pharisees hope to retain their power and their people. With our 20/20 hindsight, we can easily fall into the trap of thinking of the Pharisees as evil. But what if we were there, watching Jesus perform miracles on the Sabbath against Jewish law, hearing Jesus proclaim himself to be one with the Father? Would we drop to our knees, saying, "Yes, Lord, I believe," or would we cling to what is familiar, safe?

Believing in Jesus then meant taking a risk. Believing in Jesus today still means taking a risk. It's not easy in our secular society to openly profess what can't be proven, seen, touched with a hand. Faith requires risk as much as it requires belief. But it is often only when we take the greatest leap of faith that our hearts are most sure of what we cannot see but know to be true.

Meditation: Jesus shows us the way to convert hearts. So often it is through his actions—compassion, mercy, love—that he draws people to him. Can you do the same? As the old 1970s folk song says, "They'll know we are Christians by our love." Do the people you meet recognize Jesus in you through your daily actions?

Prayer: Holy Spirit, give us the courage we need to take a leap of faith, even when it's scary or uncomfortable. Help us to live our beliefs in both word and action so we may show others the transforming power of Jesus' love at work in everyday lives.

Beyond Calculation

Readings: Isa 42:1-7; John 12:1-11

Scripture:
Mary took a liter of costly perfumed oil
    made from genuine aromatic nard
    and anointed the feet of Jesus and dried them with her
        hair;
    the house was filled with the fragrance of the oil.
Then Judas the Iscariot . . . said,
    "Why was this oil not sold for three hundred days'
        wages
    and given to the poor?" (John 12:3-6)

Reflection: Imagine how much courage it must have required for Mary to pour expensive oil over Jesus' feet as her dinner guests looked on in confusion or consternation or outright indignation. And yet so moved was she by the presence of Jesus in her midst that she did not stop to count the cost—financial or otherwise—of her actions. She poured without measure. She poured until the entire house was filled with fragrance. She poured even as Judas tried to make her unbridled devotion seem like wasteful indiscretion.

When I read today's gospel, a more modern, gospel-inspired story came to mind, that of Dorothy Day and the diamond. One day a donor came into the Catholic Worker house in New York and gave Dorothy a diamond ring. With a simple word of thanks, she put it in her pocket. Later that day, when one of the "regulars" came in, Dorothy gave her the ring, no strings attached. Some of the volunteers were shocked, saying they could have sold the ring and paid the woman's rent for years. Dorothy responded, "Well, if she wants to sell the ring and go to the Bahamas, she can do so. But she might also like to just wear the ring. Do you think God made diamonds just for the rich?"

Like Mary in today's gospel, Dorothy did not stop to calculate the value of the ring or how she might maximize its worth. She gave without measure, moved by the awareness of God present among the people she served. True charity does not come with conditions. True faith does not count the cost.

Meditation: Imagine yourself in Mary's shoes today. What would it take to make you abandon all pretense and pour yourself out before Jesus? What holds you back? Do you let the opinions of others influence how much of yourself you are willing to give?

Prayer: Jesus, we want to give you our all, but it's hard to let go. Help us to be more like Mary, giving our heart without keeping a tally in our head. Anoint us with your Spirit, as she anointed you with perfumed oil.

The Walls Selfishness Builds

Readings: Isa 49:1-6; John 13:21-33, 36-38

Scripture:
So Judas took the morsel and left at once. And it was night. (John 13:30)

Reflection: "And it was night." That one short line at the end of today's gospel carries such weight. You can almost feel the enveloping darkness, the evening's black sky melding with Judas's black actions to create a dark night of the soul like no other. "Satan entered him," we are told. It doesn't get much darker than that.

Despite being one of Jesus' close followers, seeing his works up close, hearing his words day after day, Judas had spiritual tunnel vision; he could not see beyond his own personal ambition and agenda.

How often do we get caught up in ideas or causes, passions or projects that numb our conscience and dull our spiritual senses? Like Judas, albeit in a less dramatic way, we convince ourselves that the end justifies the means, even if the means goes against everything we profess to believe, everything we know in our hearts is right.

In a daily meditation in 2013, Pope Francis zeroed in on this very danger, saying that those who "isolate their conscience in selfishness," as Judas did, do not know how to live life as a gift. When we choose the self-centered route, he said, we insulate ourselves from the sense of community that grounds us and from the love that Jesus offers us.

We see only our own goals in the distance, and we lose sight of the path to God because it's hidden behind a wall of desires we have built up around us. Today's gospel is a sobering reminder that we need to tear down those walls of selfishness before it's too late, not little by little, brick by brick, but all at once, imploding our idols and reducing our personal agendas to rubble so the light can find its way back into our lives and our hearts as the dust settles.

Meditation: Is there anything in your life right now that is isolating you from your family or faith community? Have you convinced yourself that your actions are good and true, even though they may be hurting someone else, or hurting your relationship with God? What step can you take today to reclaim truth in your life, to knock down the walls you've built?

Prayer: Forgiving Father, we know we have made mistakes and have placed our own selfish wants and desires ahead of you. Give us the grace today and always to live life as a gift.

Patched Together with Love

Readings: Isa 50:4-9a; Matt 26:14-25

Scripture:
   "What are you willing to give me
   if I hand him over to you?"
They paid him thirty pieces of silver. (Matt 26:15)

Reflection: Betrayal. We cannot escape it this week. Judas whispers in our ear day after day, reminding us that we are not as safe or free from deep sin as we might like to think. "Surely it is not I, Rabbi?" Judas says to Jesus, even after he has just struck a bargain for his life, or at least for his arrest.

We know not long after this exchange, Judas will realize what he's done, and he will misjudge Jesus for a second time, in the most painful and misguided way. He will choose suicide over mercy, which surely would have been his if he had but gone to Jesus and asked for forgiveness. We know that without question, that mercy would have been freely given to Judas, as it was to the "good thief" on the cross.

Do we recognize that this same limitless mercy is freely given to us as well, any time and every time we sin and repent? If not, we, too, run the risk of misjudging Jesus and taking justice and condemnation into our own hands. While on the surface, that kind of self-effacement might seem like humility, it is in fact ego talking because we do not want to admit our brokenness to ourselves, to those around us, even to God, who longs to make us whole.

There is a Japanese art form known as Kintsukuroi, which is used to repair broken pottery. Instead of gluing the pots back together with invisible glue to hide the damage, the cracks are filled with silver or gold, making them more beautiful and more valuable than before they were broken.

God is like that with us. If we are willing to put ego away and seek forgiveness, he will fill our cracks with his love and transform our brokenness into something more beautiful than we could ever imagine.

Meditation: What are the cracks in your life that need filling? How have you tried to patch the pieces together on your own? Is it working? What would happen if you bared your soul before God and allowed him to put you back together?

Prayer: Abba Father, you are the potter and we are the clay. Take our broken pieces and make us whole once again. Give us the humility to come to you for mercy, even when we think that we, like Judas, are beyond repair, beyond redemption.

Entering the Mystery

Readings: Exod 12:1-8, 11-14; 1 Cor 11:23-26; John 13:1-15

Scripture:
"I have given you a model to follow,
  so that as I have done for you, you should also do."
    (John 13:15)

Reflection: Taken as a whole, today's readings can feel too big, too overwhelming. Where should we focus our hearts and minds? On the Eucharist? The institution of the priest-hood? The prediction of Judas's betrayal? The washing of feet? There are so many significant things here, things that will not only influence the events of the next few days but will alter the course of history for all time. Running through everything, however, are powerful undercurrents, less obvi-ous but no less significant for us.

"Jesus knew that his hour had come to pass from this world to the Father. He loved his own in the world and he loved them to the end," we hear at the opening of the gospel. "He loved his own . . ." We are his own, even when we, like Peter during the washing of the feet, don't understand what the Lord is asking of us; even when we, like Judas, actively choose to do something to break our relationship with God. Jesus loved them—and us—to the end, despite mistakes and weaknesses and outright rejection. It's what he calls each of us to do: to love others despite their weaknesses, to serve others even when we'd rather be served, to follow the model he set for us.

In Jesus' example we see all of the seemingly disparate and overwhelming pieces of today's Scripture coming together. Jesus does the Father's will even when he had the power to change his course. He allows himself not only to be broken for us but given to us as an ongoing source of comfort, grace, and spiritual nourishment in the Eucharist. Jesus does not wait to be served but rushes into the void to care for others. Trust, sacrifice, service. Can we do as he did, follow where he leads?

Meditation: Today marks the beginning of the Sacred Triduum. We enter into these days with a solemn silence in our hearts, even as we go about our daily business. Take time today, tonight, to step outside your routine and dwell in the mystery that remains so powerful to this day even though we know the outcome.

Prayer: Jesus, Bread of Life, our souls hunger for the spiritual food that only you can provide. As we mark the celebration of the first Eucharist, we give thanks for the gift of yourself that nourishes us for the journey ahead.

A Kiss of Gratitude

Readings: Isa 52:13–53:12; Heb 4:14-16; 5:7-9; John 18:1–19:42

Scripture:
When Jesus had taken the wine, he said,
    "It is finished."
And bowing his head, he handed over the spirit.
    (John 19:30)

Reflection: Every Good Friday, I am transported back, in my mind's eye, to the gymnasium that served as my parish church when I was growing up. I was probably about sixteen years old on this particular Good Friday, sitting in an uncomfortable metal folding chair at what would have been center court if I'd been aiming for the basketball net over the altar. But none of those odd physical details really mattered to me. What mattered, what makes the memory of that day so powerful more than thirty-five years later, is the fact that I remember listening to the homily with tears streaming down my face.

I can't recall what was said that moved me so deeply. I just remember that on that one Good Friday I could not contain my sorrow and awe over what Jesus did for me. Every year since, I have wondered how it's possible that I'm not crying or, at the very least, kneeling before the cross in fear and trembling. How is it possible that the crucifixion and what it meant for the people then and for me today has become so "normal" that it does not leave me gasping with gratitude? How do I pass by the crosses hanging in my parish church and my own home without a second glance, without so much as a prayerful nod?

Pope Francis, during his second Holy Week as pope, gave Catholics a simple instruction: Take a crucifix and kiss it throughout the day, saying, "Thank you, Jesus. Thank you, Lord." So simple, and yet so powerful that we just might find ourselves coming back to the practice year after year with tears in our eyes.

Meditation: How often do you stop to contemplate the crucifix? Have you allowed yourself to become numb to the meaning of this transforming moment in our salvation? Today, as we read the Lord's passion, can you place yourself at the foot of the cross and see this act of pure love with new eyes?

Prayer: Lamb of God, you took away the sins of the world through the gift of your body broken on the cross. We know we are not worthy of this sacrifice, and yet we are so grateful for the mercy and love you poured out for us on Calvary and which continue to pour out each time you are broken for us in the Eucharist.

Waiting in the Shadows

Readings: Gen 1:1–2:2; Gen 22:1-18; Exod 14:15–15:1; Isa 54:5-14; Isa 55:1-11; Bar 3:9-15, 32–4:4; Ezek 36:16-17a, 18-28; Rom 6:3-11; Luke 24:1-12

Scripture:
"Why do you seek the living one among the dead?"
  (Luke 24:5b)

Reflection: I've been awake since 4:30 a.m., which seems appropriate somehow on this day of watching and waiting. The rain is coming down. The sun has not made an appearance. It is as if the world is weeping and holding its breath all at once, waiting for an answer.

At this point in the season, past the Lenten promises—too many of them unfulfilled—I usually identify with Peter, locked away, afraid, ashamed, alone. Every year I start out wanting Lent to be "perfect." And, every year, as if on cue, I am astounded by my own weaknesses by the time Holy Saturday arrives.

The forty days leading up to this moment often don't turn out as planned. Sick children and busy work projects, school vacations and flooded basements can keep us down, both physically and spiritually, for days and weeks on end. We watch our plans unravel and feel like failures because we are focused on our own expectations rather than the realities

God has in store. Like Peter hiding in fear and guilt or the women rushing from the tomb in fear and confusion, we can lose sight of God's grace right before our eyes and spend our lives in a fruitless search for the "living one among the dead."

Today, as we wait in darkness for the light that will break into our world just as the sun starts to fade, we can remember that things often are not as they appear. Like the earliest disciples broken by what seemed like defeat on the cross, we, too, are often broken by what appears on the surface to be failure. But perhaps our "failures" are just different, albeit bumpier, paths to the same truth.

On this Holy Saturday, many of us wait in shadows of our own making, like Peter, longing to be set free.

Meditation: How often do you lock yourself away in fear—literally and figuratively—from things that scare you? What do you gain from it? Imagine yourself as one of the first disciples. How would you have felt on the first Holy Saturday? What would have gone through your mind when you found an empty tomb?

Prayer: God of new life, as we keep silent vigil today, give us the wisdom to recognize the graces that are ours when we let go of expectations, let go of fears, and trust in your promises.

New Beginnings, New Life

Readings: Acts 10:34a, 37-43; Col 3:1-4 or 1 Cor 5:6b-8; John 20:1-9 or Luke 24:1-12

Scripture:
Then the other disciple also went in,
    the one who had arrived at the tomb first,
    and he saw and believed. (John 20:8)

Reflection: Alleluia, Alleluia. He is risen! After the difficult journey to Calvary and the long hours of waiting, those words feel like a beautiful spring breeze blowing through my soul and clearing out the last vestiges of darkness and fear. Do you feel it? Breathe deep of our new life in Christ! With the Good News of Easter Sunday, everything is changed. Life is changed. Death is changed. We are changed.

In today's gospel, Mary Magdalene, Peter, and the "disciple whom Jesus loved" confront the emptiness of the tomb, just as we do today, with excitement that is tinged with mystery and trepidation. What does the empty tomb mean for them, for us? They believed, we are told, although they did not yet understand.

It sounds familiar, doesn't it? We, too, believe even though we will probably never fully understand the miracle of the resurrection this side of heaven. How could we? Our God defeated death, transforming the cross from a symbol of suffering into a symbol of salvation, resurrection, and eternal life.

It's not easy for our minds to grasp things so utterly incomprehensible on a human scale, and yet we believe, we celebrate. At Mass, we attempt to make a leap toward that heavenly mystery in concrete earthly ways, through fire and water, incense and song. We let Alleluias ring out for the first time in weeks in a verbal burst of joy that cannot begin to express our gratitude and awe. Although we've been here before, it is as if we are hearing it all for the first time. The tomb is empty! Run, and tell everyone you meet.

Life begins again today. Even without dying, we feel reborn because we have been given the ultimate second chance. Without earning it, without understanding it, resurrection is now our destiny. Never has emptiness felt so full.

Alleluia. Alleluia. He is risen. And we are saved.

Meditation: Churches are overflowing with flowers, overflowing with people, overflowing with joy today. We are Easter people. How will today's Good News manifest itself in your daily life? What will be different? How are you changed? What does the empty tomb mean to you?

Prayer: Risen Lord, we sing your praise today as we celebrate your resurrection and the salvation you have won for us. Make us worthy to share in your eternal life.

References

Introduction
Pope Francis, Message of His Holiness Pope Francis for Lent 2015, Libreria Editrice Vaticana, October 4, 2014, https://w2
.vatican.va/content/francesco/en/messages/lent/documents
/papa-francesco_20141004_messaggio-quaresima2015.html.

February 19: Friday of the First Week of Lent
Carol Glatz, "Words can kill: Murder and insults are both rooted in hatred, says pope," *Catholic News Service*, June 12, 2014, http://www.catholicnews.com/data/stories/cns
/1402412.htm.

February 20: Saturday of the First Week of Lent
Dorothy Day, *On Pilgrimage* (Grand Rapids, MI: Eerdmans, 1999), 122.

February 26: Friday of the Second Week of Lent
Henri Nouwen, *The Return of the Prodigal Son* (New York: Doubleday, 1994), 85.

March 3: Thursday of the Third Week of Lent
Norvene Vest, *No Moment Too Small: Rhythms of Silence, Prayer & Holy Reading* (Lanham, MD: Rowman & Littlefield, 2008), 15, 17.

March 6: Fourth Sunday of Lent
Margaret Silf, *Wayfaring: A Gospel Journey in Everyday Life* (Notre Dame, IN: Ave Maria Press, 2009), 62.

March 10: Thursday of the Fourth Week of Lent
Elizabeth Scalia, *Strange Gods: Unmasking the Idols in Everyday Life* (Notre Dame, IN: Ave Maria Press, 2013), 10.

March 14: Monday of the Fifth Week of Lent
Walter Ciszek, *He Leadeth Me: An Extraordinary Testament of Faith* (New York: Random House, 1973), 87.

March 21: Monday of Holy Week
Jim Forest, "Work Hard, Pray Hard: On Dorothy Day and Thomas Merton," *U.S. Catholic*, November 2010, http://www.uscatholic.org/culture/social-justice/2011/09/work-hard-pray-hard-dorthy-day-and-thomas-merton.

March 22: Tuesday of Holy Week
Carol Glatz, "Pope: Satan tricks people into being selfish, leaving them loveless," *Catholic News Service*, May 14, 2013, http://www.catholicnews.com/data/stories/cns/1302131.htm.